A LOO WITH
A VIEW

A LOO WITH A VIEW

Luke Barclay

FIREFLY BOOKS

A FIREFLY BOOK

Published by Firefly Books Ltd. 2011

Copyright © 2011 Luke Barclay

First printing

Publisher Cataloging-in-Publication Data (U.S.)
Barclay, Luke.
A loo with a view : sights you can see from the comfort of a convenience / Luke Barclay.
[176] p. : col. photos. ; cm.
Summary: Photographs of the world's most scenic cisterns and panoramic
privies, from a Buddhist monastery in India to the peak of Mount Kilimanjaro.
ISBN-13: 978-1-55407-901-8
1. Toilets – Pictorial works. 2. Public toilets – Pictorial works. 3. Restrooms –
Pictorial works. I. Title.
728/.9 dc22   GT476.B3745 2011

Library and Archives Canada Cataloguing in Publication
Barclay, Luke
A loo with a view : sights you can see from the comfort of a convenience / Luke Barclay.
ISBN 978-1-55407-901-8

1. Toilets--Pictorial works. 2. Public toilets--Pictorial
works. 3. Restrooms--Pictorial works. I. Title.

GT476.B37 2011   696'.1820222   C2011-900752-5

Published in the United States by
Firefly Books (U.S.) Inc.
P.O. Box 1338, Ellicott Station
Buffalo, New York 14205

Published in Canada by
Firefly Books Ltd.
66 Leek Crescent
Richmond Hill, Ontario L4B 1H1

Cover design: Christine Rae

Printed in China

Contents

Introduction

Many years ago, on a family holiday, I found myself sitting on a loo in the upstairs bathroom of a seaside cottage. As I sat doing my thing, a well-placed window offered views of an ancient chapel in a field on the cliff top with ocean waves breaking on the rocks below. It was my first experience of a loo with a view — an exhilarating, heart-pounding, life-changing moment.

A few years later, while sitting on another loo (which only had a view of a bath) I made a promise to myself. My mission was simple. I would seek out and document the world's best loos with views. It has been quite a journey. Considering the amount of loitering I have done in toilets with a camera, it is a miracle that I'm not in prison.

According to the World Toilet Organization (there really is one), we spend around three years of our lives in the bathroom. That is a long time to be sitting and staring at a door. Answering the call of nature should be uplifting and entertaining, thought-provoking and enlightening. It can be.

When I set out on my quest, I thought I was alone. But along the way I have been helped by countless people from all over the world, who have sent me toilet tip-offs and photographs. Together, we form a small but enthusiastic global community — undivided by class, race or religion — united by a love of loos that have views.

Writing a book about views from toilets, I feared the worst. Was I going to be labelled as some kind of toilet-obsessed freak? But then the magic began - a gentleman in Bangalore, India, reads about my search in his morning paper and sends a fantastic photo of a urinal in the Himalayas; a young British fashion designer vows to "find a loo with a view if it kills me" on a trip to South America and discovers three; and an architect reads my book and decides to add views to his bathroom designs.

There's no denying it, the world is embracing loos with views — from open-air loos in National Parks, to urinals in front of windows, to composting toilets on tropical islands, to toilet blocks on the summits of sacred mountains. It is clear that the journey has only just begun.

Luke Barclay
loos@looswithviews.com

THE LOOS

Boulder Pass Campsite

Glacier National Park, Montana, United States

View: the world at its most beautiful and most fragile

You sit enthroned – exposed, alone and exhilarated – at one with nature. For loo-view purists this is what it is all about. No protection, no sinks, no soap dispensers. It is just you, a loo and a spectacular view.

The loo (photographed with the lid down), is known as a "low rider" – a simple wooden box with a seat, designed to sit on ground in which it is difficult to dig a pit. And there is certainly plenty to keep your mind occupied whilst using it – as you look out at the Agassiz Glacier; it is frightening to think that in 1850 the glacier covered some four square kilometers (1.54 sqaure miles), but by 1993 had shrunk to just one (0.39 square miles).

Open-air toilets offer some of the most exhilarating and thought-provoking loo experiences on the planet. They are out there waiting to be used and enjoyed. So get out of your bathroom, get into the wild (taking all appropriate precautions) and go find yourself a low rider.

Mount Fuji

Central Honshū, Japan

View: unforgettable toileting – see Japan awake beneath you from the summit loo

They climb through the night in the thousands to see the sun rise over the land of the rising sun. And waiting on the summit at over 12,000 feet is a post office, a restaurant, vending machines selling hot coffee and, of course, state-of-the-art toilets.

This is a spotlessly clean, fully flushable, unisex facility. And with each cubicle boasting its own window, it is a loo with a view that everyone can enjoy.

Incredibly, reports suggest that atmospheric music from the restaurant can sometimes be heard from the stalls – creating one of the world's great loo experiences. As English tourist Sam Jones explained: "I stood at the urinal looking at a silhouetted Shinto shrine, while listening to Aerosmith's 'I Don't Wanna Miss a Thing' – it was awesome!"

Visiting Fuji is a pilgrimage for the Japanese. There are numerous toilets on the mountain to serve the 200,000 or so who climb each year. The price of using one rises with altitude, peaking at 200 yen. A brave band of attendants live on the mountain to maintain standards.

N Seoul Tower

Seoul, South Korea

View: good for the "Seoul" – stand and see a city beneath your feet

The urinals in Seoul Tower's "Sky Restrooms" are purpose-built loos with views – part of a new wave that is reinventing the indoor toilet experience. All too often dank, windowless and depressing, this is the way it ought to be.

They offer a near picture-perfect view of the South Korean capital. For those who step up to the plate it is an unforgettable, uplifting and reaffirming experience. "I feel ten feet tall," said one user. "I'm back," said another.

Seoul Tower stands proud on top of Mount Namsan. It was refurbished and reopened in 2005 and branded as the "N Seoul Tower." The N stands for both "new" and "Namsan."

Reports suggest that the "Sky Restrooms" are advertised in the tower's elevator. It is a happy day when a toilet becomes a tourist attraction in its own right.

The ladies' restroom also has a view – from the sinks. Now that is a great hand wash.

Cliff-Top Chateau

View: contemplate your future above a bend in the Dordogne River

The humble toilet is a sanctuary – an island of calm in a sea of stress. Away from the pressures of the world, it is the perfect place to escape and find distance, the perfect place to sit and ponder.

And located in a cliff-top French chateau with a view of one of the world's most picturesque rivers, this WC is, arguably, the most relaxing and thought-provoking toilet on Earth. When it comes to philosophizing on the loo it does not get any better than this.

Rivers have long been seen as a metaphor for life. They have a beginning and an end. They are filled with twists and turns, as well as hidden dangers (e.g. anacondas). They can flow quickly or slowly, you can try to steer a course or allow yourself to go with the flow. But whatever happens, a river will keep on flowing (except during a severe drought) and you never know what's around the next bend.

The bathroom has recently been renovated and the position of the toilet reversed, no doubt to counter the neck-ache caused by years of looking left.

As well as providing an insight into the nature of life, the Dordogne is also popular with canoeists.

Croagh Patrick

County Mayo, Ireland

View: divine – as you exit, the view from the mountain appears in all its magnificent glory

Situated on the summit of sacred Croagh Patrick in the west of Ireland, this loo is a haven for walkers and pilgrims alike. And using it is certainly quite an experience – to have the chance to relieve yourself after the long climb and then be greeted by this wondrous view is absolute heaven on Earth.

This could well be the world's holiest toilet block. In AD 441, it is said that St Patrick fasted on the summit for forty days and forty nights. It was from here that he supposedly banished all snakes from Ireland – a legend steeped in religious symbolism, with the serpents representing paganism, as there were no snakes in the first place.

Today, in memory of St Patrick's fast, thousands of Catholic pilgrims climb the mountain on the last Sunday of July, known as "Reek Sunday." Many even climb barefoot to show penitence.

Discovering a loo on the summit is quite a relief and quite a surprise. As one pilgrim commented: "Oh blimey, it's a toilet."

Mount Sinai

Sinai Peninsula, Egypt

View: see the stunning mountains of Sinai through gaps in the bamboo

It might seem crazy, but the best place to see the sunrise on Mount Sinai is from inside this toilet. The early-morning light is said to flood in through the bamboo, revealing the view to those seated within. It is a once-in-a-lifetime opportunity – so uplifting that it could drive a man to poetry. This is a place to see your future, a place to have an epiphany, a place to find peace.

Mount Sinai is a popular destination with both pilgrims and tourists. In the Old Testament it is said to be where Moses was handed the Ten Commandments by God. The Bedouin even call the mountain Jabal Musa, meaning "Moses Mountain." However, the actual location of the biblical Mount Sinai is still open to debate.

Climbers battle against freezing temperatures and icy winds to be at the summit for sunrise. Some come more prepared than others – tourists have even been known to climb in high-heeled shoes. It is not thought that this choice of footwear carries any particular religious significance.

Tengboche Monastery

View: a happy day – the highest point on Earth from a loo

The rare photograph on the right is one of the few images ever captured of Mount Everest as seen from a toilet. It was taken on January 1, 2000 at the Tengboche Monastery, high in the Nepalese Himalayas. What a way to start a new millennium!

Facilities may be basic – a hole in the ground above a pit and bring-your-own paper. However, any loo that has a view of the highest point on Earth has to be up there as one of the greatest and most exciting on the planet.

And like many great toilets, it invites us to pause and reflect. For example: at the dawn of the next century chances are that this view will be unchanged – still serene, peaceful, magnificent and pure. However, in what state will the world that lies beneath it be?

Tengboche Monastery is an important spiritual center for the Sherpa people. The surrounding area is a refuge for wildlife – in keeping with the Buddhist principle of peace and compassion, no animal can be hunted or killed.

The peak of Everest appears at the top left of the window.

Ryoshi Restaurant

Tirtagangga, Bali, Indonesia

View: serene – sit, relax and observe life in this tranquil Balinese village

I had traveled for over twenty-four hours to reach his loo and as I approached the restaurant Wayan came out to greet me. He smiled, gave me a hug and simply said: "You came." A memorable moment and a memorable loo!

Tirtagangga is a small Balinese rice-farming community. As you sit in this open-fronted hero of a toilet, watching the world go by, it is fascinating to think about the co-operative farming methods being used in the paddy fields below. For centuries Balinese farmers have worked together to try to ensure their collective survival. Individuals belong to organizations called *subaks*, which oversee the even distribution of water to all members.

The *subak* system means that water flows down the mountains and through the terraced paddy fields of Bali, even reaching the farmers at the very bottom. The Balinese have turned their mountains into level playing fields.

As well as coming to see Tirtagangga's loo with a view, it is also worth visiting the village to bathe in its holy waters, which are said to have healing and anti-aging powers.

The Valley of Longevity

Vilcabamba, Ecuador

View: the secret of eternal youth?

It is easy to forget that the way we live can directly affect the age at which we die. It is important to stop and consider this and there is nowhere more appropriate than on this splendid wooden long-drop, located high in the Ecuadorian Andes near the village of Vilcabamba.

Meaning "sacred valley" in the Incan Quichua dialect, Vilcabamba has become famous for the extraordinary lifespan of its population. It is said that in the "valley of longevity" many have lived well into their hundreds – there have even been rumors of individuals living to 135.

Vilcabamba's secret has been the source of much study, discussion and debate. Various theories have been put forward to explain the incredible lifespan of the population – everything from the mineral balance of the water, to the balanced climate, to the suggestion that the people of Vilcabamba can't count!

Whatever the truth, no one has yet considered that the secret could lie in the uplifting effects of open-air loos in the region. And it is about time that this theory was given the attention it deserves.

Terminal 3

Singapore Changi Airport, Singapore

View: flight SQ2 to San Francisco, via Hong Kong, prepares for boarding

There's a buzz of excitement at the urinals between Gates B6 and B7. The toilet attendant is looking extremely proud. The new Airbus A380 has just taxied past the window.

For plane-spotters, these urinals are a dream come true – to be able to pursue a hobby while answering nature's call is a real privilege. "The only thing better than that would have been to see Concorde's final landing from a loo," said one spotter.

It remains to be seen whether plane-spotting from toilets takes off within the wider spotting community. However, with reports that there are loos with views in at least two other international airports, Vienna and Stockholm-Arlanda, there has to be a chance.

Terminal 3 at Singapore Changi Airport opened in January 2008. It is exciting to think that this could be the future in airport toileting.

As well as offering views of planes being loaded and unloaded, taxiing to and from the runway and even taking off and landing, these urinals each feature a small painted fly in the receptacle, which helps users with their aim.

Alcatraz Guard Tower

Alcatraz Island, San Francisco Bay, California

View: on the job, guards had panoramic vistas of San Francisco Bay

No wonder escape from Alcatraz was considered near impossible. Security at the notorious prison was so tight that guards could even watch for break-outs when they were using the loo.

Look carefully and you can spot a toilet in the remaining guard tower. It offered unobstructed, 360-degree views of the island and San Francisco Bay. There were once several towers on Alcatraz and, although shifts in them could be long, lonely and laborious, the loo views were out of this world.

Alcatraz housed many of America's most notorious criminals, including Al Capone. Prisoners had toilets in their cells. Some faced windows, offering a tantalizing glimpse of the free world through the bars. There must have been some serious escape plotting done on those loos!

Its location amidst the freezing waters and strong currents of San Francisco Bay made "the rock" as secure as they come. In its twenty-nine-year history (1934–1963) there were fourteen escape attempts. None were successful, although five prisoners are still unaccounted for. It is assumed that they drowned in the bay. But did they?

Livingstone Island

View: "the smoke that thunders"

In November 1855, on one of his great African adventures, Dr David Livingstone traveled by canoe to an island in the middle of the Zambezi River and became the first European to set eyes on what they called the "Mosi-oa-Tunya" or "the smoke that thunders." He had just "discovered" Victoria Falls, which he named in honor of Queen Victoria.

Now, over 150 years later, it is possible to sit on a toilet literally meters from the edge of this magnificent waterfall and relive the very moment of Livingstone's find. It is not often that you can sit on a loo and know that you are following in the footsteps of history.

Dr Livingstone's discovery was made during a transcontinental expedition across Africa – a journey that would secure his fame.

While on a later expedition to trace the source of the Nile, Livingstone lost contact with the outside world and Henry Morton Stanley was famously sent by the *New York Herald* to track him down. On doing so he is said to have let out the immortal words: "Dr Livingstone, I presume?"

Top-Secret Tunnels

Dover Castle, Dover, United Kingdom

View: a window in the white cliffs offers views of Dover Harbor

In 1940 the view from this loo was very different – thousands of troops returning home from the beaches of Dunkirk in one of the most audacious rescue missions of all time. This loo has seen it all. Here is a loo that is part of history.

It can be found in tunnels hidden in the white cliffs beneath Dover Castle. Dug during the Napoleonic Wars and modernized as war with Hitler loomed, it was in these tunnels that Vice-Admiral Ramsay masterminded "Operation Dynamo," the famous Dunkirk evacuation in which 338,000 troops were saved from the jaws of the enemy to fight another day.

Winston Churchill came to Dover prior to the evacuation, although it is not known whether he visited this loo and enjoyed the view. Workers in the tunnels certainly did – it was one of the only places from which you could see the outside world.

Eight years after Dunkirk, this loo must have offered a view of the Olympic torch as it arrived in Britain for the 1948 London Olympics at Wembley – a symbol of hope after a long and bloody war.

Copeland Bird Observatory

Copeland Island, County Down, Northern Ireland

View: birds through binoculars

Visiting the loo is a great way of spending some "alone time" – getting back in touch with yourself and what makes you happy. Therefore, in an ideal world, it ought to be possible to continue pursuing your passions from the toilet. Admittedly some hobbies are more straightforward than others – reading and knitting are clearly easier than fishing or snooker – but the principle is there.

And so bravo to the Copeland Bird Observatory! Using a traditional Irish half-door, they have devised a system that not only respects privacy and protects honor, but also allows members and visitors to the island to carry on their ornithological pursuits.

Built in 1979 and soon to be given a new stone-clad finish, you can sense the love that has gone into making this toilet what it is today. And the plumbing is ingenious – the flush uses water from a nearby well, while waste is taken away through a twenty-meter pipe down into the sea. Members claim that the lobsters in the water below the pipe are the biggest in the area. Win-win!

One Tree Island Research Station

The Great Barrier Reef, Australia

View: nature at its most beautiful and brutal

Many would argue that a solar-powered island in a lagoon on the Great Barrier Reef is as good as it gets. However, as good as it gets just got better. Here is a solar-powered island in a lagoon on the Great Barrier Reef that has a toilet from which you can see a colony of Black Noddy terns – mating.

For bird-watching enthusiasts this composting toilet is paradise on Earth – members of the Copeland Bird Observatory would surely relish the chance to use it. In January adult terns care for eggs and chicks. Sadly, strong winds and rain cause their young to fall from the nests, where they are eaten by seagulls and egrets.

Black Noddy terns build their nests from dried leaves covered in their own droppings. A comforting thought as you sit on a composting toilet knowing that your droppings are about to be recycled into fertilizer. Talk about renewable waste!

Lords

View: perfectly framed – the wicket at the home of cricket

Visiting the loo while watching live sport is a dangerous game. What if you had been stuck in the toilet at the Nou Camp in 1999 as Ole Gunnar Solskjær won the European Cup for Manchester United? It is a sickening thought.

However, in the Warner Stand at Lords, gents (sorry, ladies) can visit the loo safe in the knowledge that they will not miss a single ball. Lords is the home of cricket. It is also the home of the best-placed window in the entire world.

Imagine the great sporting moments that must have been seen from these urinals! To have watched Andrew Strauss reach a century on his test debut would certainly have been quite something, while witnessing any moment of Graham Gooch's famous innings of 333 against India in 1990 would arguably have been the best toilet experience of all time.

Other stadia around the world rumored to have loos with views are the Antigua Recreation Ground, the M.C.G. in Melbourne and New Lodge – home of Billericay Town Football Club, Essex.

"miX Lounge"

Mandalay Bay, Las Vegas, Nevada

View: Interstate 15 leaves Las Vegas

When it comes to views from public loos, users of seated toilets (very often women) undoubtedly get a raw deal. It is an unacceptable imbalance in the system. While urinals are frequently found in front of windows, in the stalls you find yourself looking at your feet, reading graffiti or staring at a door.

But not in Vegas, baby! Facing a floor-to-ceiling window made from one-way glass, the functional just became phenomenal. While the "miX Lounge" itself looks out over the Strip, its loos offer an alternative view. Sit and watch cars leaving Las Vegas on Interstate Highway 15 as it heads off south towards Los Angeles.

North to south, Interstate 15 runs from the Canadian border in Montana right through to San Diego, California. If you were to take a road trip on this highway you would not only hit Las Vegas, where you can visit one of the world's best restrooms, but would also see the "world's tallest thermometer" (134 feet) in Baker, California (also the "Gateway to Death Valley"), surely worth the 2,306-kilometer (1,433-mile) journey in itself?

Dune 45, Sossusvlei

Namib-Naukluft National Park, Namib Desert, Namibia

View: arid – one of the world's highest sand dunes in one of the oldest deserts on Earth

On the surface, this fine wooden latrine, located in the shadow of a magnificent sand dune deep in the Namib Desert, and the former England football manager Graham Taylor have absolutely nothing in common. Incredibly, however, there is a link. In 2001, a PhD student working in Namibia named a sand dune the "G Taylor Dune" in honor of his hero.

In 1994, a British documentary captured a team talk given by Taylor prior to a crucial game against the Netherlands, in which he spoke about the world being full of opportunities and how life's winners tended to be those who seek out and see opportunities and then take them.

England lost 2–0 and Taylor lost his job. However, his sentiments resound as you look out at this immense pile of shifting sand – constantly moving and evolving, constantly being shaped by the wind. How will the wind shape you? What opportunities will it blow your way? Will you see them and will you take them?

Close to the Salar de Uyuni

Andean High Plateau, Bolivia

View: beautifully arid landscape and a mini salt desert

Heated toilet seats, air fresheners and fancy soap are all well and good. But it is the simple things in life that have the power to make us truly happy. As one user of this stunning latrine commented: "The toilets are quite simple, just a hole … but the scenery is so beautiful that I wouldn't trade any golden bathroom for this one." Amen.

It is located in the Andean High Plateau, just around the corner from the famous Salar de Uyuni – a gigantic sea of salt (the largest in the world), which stretches for thousands of square kilometers. The Salar de Uyuni was formed when a prehistoric lake dried to leave two new lakes and two huge salt flats, the larger being Uyuni.

It has been estimated that Uyuni contains ten billion tons of salt. A trip to this loo, with its considerably smaller salt plain, offers a charming glimpse of what lies ahead or reminds you that what you have just seen was not a dream.

Djankuat Glacier Research Station

Caucasus Mountains, Russia

View: a shrinking glacier and the highest mountain in Europe

Many outdoor loos without locks have novel "engaged" systems to prevent embarrassment. And the one in place for this toilet is particularly fitting. Amazingly, occupants must leave the toilet door open to signify to others that it is being used. This system not only works, it also creates a loo with a view of the highest mountain in Europe.

The loo belongs to a research station, that lies deep within the Caucasus Mountains. The views are both significant and stunning. The last thing you see before entering is the Djankuat Glacier, one of UNESCO's reference glaciers for monitoring climate change. And inside the engaged system ensures a terrific view of Mount Elbrus.

During the Second World War, German soldiers scaled Elbrus and placed a Nazi flag on the summit, although it was later removed by the Soviets. Thinking back to this moment and with the image of the melting glacier still fresh in your mind, you are reminded of man's impact on the course of history and our ability to damage as well as save the planet on which we live.

Boston Basin High Camp

North Cascades National Park, Washington

View: strong all-rounder – an uninterrupted view of Johannesburg Mountain

If you were to construct a score sheet to evaluate the standard of loos that have views, it would include the following questions:

1. Can you see the view while actually using the loo?
2. Can both men and women use it?
3. How easy is it to see the view, e.g. is a head swivel necessary?
4. How good is the view?
5. How interesting and/or thought-provoking is the view?
6. Is the view unobstructed? (a wall, tree, fence or bush might block the line of sight)
7. How user-friendly is the loo?
8. What is the overall impact on the user?

While the answers to some questions are of course subjective, few would disagree that the Boston Basin loo scores well in almost every area. A spectacular, unspoiled, uninterrupted, sweeping vista lies directly in front of you while seated – and for added entertainment it is even located near a colony of marmots!

The Boston Basin privy – setting the standard for all-round excellence in loo viewing.

Spider Rock

Canyon de Chelly, Chinle, Arizona, United States

View: Spider Rock rises from the floor of this sacred Navajo canyon

It had been a long hike in baking temperatures from the rim down to the canyon floor. And suddenly there it was – awesome, beautiful and magnificent – at the base of an 800-foot sandstone spire, the best-placed family toilet on the planet.

Humans have lived in the Canyon de Chelly (pronounced "de shay") for thousands of years. The Native American Navajo people entered the canyon around 1700. And many still live here in their spiritual home today. In the summer, Navajo families move into the canyon to farm their lands and raise sheep, living in traditional-style homes, called hogans.

Although the canyon feels peaceful today, this has not always been the case. Perhaps most famously, in 1864 US forces stormed the canyon and killed or captured most of the Navajo within. Prisoners were forced to walk for over three hundred miles to Fort Sumner – known as the "Long Walk" – where they faced incarceration for the next four years before being allowed to return home.

Mount Whitney

View: absolute freedom – sit and take in the triumphant view from the summit loo

Infamous amongst the climbing community for many years, reports suggest that this toilet is sadly now no more. Where this proud, bald-headed eagle of a loo once stood, now sit only rocks. It may be gone but it will not be forgotten.

Exposed to the elements and boasting an awe-inspiring, panoramic view, this loo took toileting to a whole new level. It was a latrine with one hell of an attitude – a pumped-up, adrenalin-fuelled, roller-coaster ride of a loo.

In just one single hour screams of "awesome," "I love being me" and "man, that's good" were all heard coming from the direction of this loo. It was a toilet that made you feel free. It was a toilet that made you want to stand up and shout, "God bless America!"

At over 14,500 feet, the summit of Mount Whitney is the highest point in the contiguous United States. Amazingly, just a few hours east of this giant mountain is the lowest point in North America, eighty-six meters below sea level, at Death Valley.

Tasman Saddle Hut

Tasman Glacier, South Island, New Zealand

View: a loo from above – and on the edge

We have seen that it is possible to spot planes from toilets. However few would have believed that it is also possible to spot toilets from planes.

Taken in 1990 from high above New Zealand's Tasman Glacier, this rare archive photograph proves that it can be done. Although the loo has since been upgraded, this still stands as one of the few images ever captured of a loo from the air.

It makes you want more. Perhaps it is time for loo-spotting pleasure flights – giving the general public the opportunity to see some of the world's most remote, out-there and on-the-edge toilets. You heard it here first.

Where will the relationship between loos and planes end? There have even been reports that some airlines have windows in their upper-class toilets, theoretically making it possible to spot a loo on the ground from a loo in a plane!

Now there is a mile-high club you want to be a part of.

Mount McKinley

View: a "great one" – Mount Foraker from 14,200 feet

While observing loos from planes clearly has a lot of potential as a tourist enterprise, nothing beats getting out into the wilderness yourself and experiencing them first-hand. Only in freezing temperatures, with the wind lashing at your cheeks, can you truly appreciate the wondrous sense of escape that loos with views can provide. "Adventure toileting" – it ought to be an Olympic sport.

This image was captured in May 2006 on a successful expedition to the summit of Mount McKinley. At 20,320 feet, McKinley is the highest mountain in North America. Although the peak is nearer sea level, the mountain's rise of 18,000 feet from base to peak is far greater than that of Mount Everest.

Many prefer to call Mount McKinley by its original name, Denali, which means "great one" in the native Athapaskan language. Denali was renamed after William McKinley in 1896, shortly before he became the twenty-fifth president of the United States. President McKinley was assassinated by an anarchist in 1901 and replaced by number twenty-six, Theodore Roosevelt.

The Station Inn

Ribblehead, North Yorkshire Dales, United Kingdom

View: the famous Ribblehead Viaduct – a dream come true for trainspotters

If there was a competition for Britain's best view from a pub urinal, the left-hand installation at the Station Inn would be odds-on favorite. With a clear view of a magnificent twenty-four-arch railway viaduct, this is pub toileting at its most exhilarating.

The Ribblehead Viaduct is the iconic image of the Settle–Carlisle Railway. It was constructed in the early 1870s – part of the nineteenth-century railway boom, which transformed the face of Britain and the world.

Thousands of "navvies," who built the viaduct largely by hand, lived in shanty towns on the moor during the years of construction. Many workers and members of their families were killed in industrial accidents and smallpox epidemics. Over 200 are buried in a nearby churchyard.

Using the urinal while a train is crossing the viaduct can be the cause of tremendous excitement at the inn. As railway enthusiast Lawrence Knowles exclaimed: "Lads, I've just seen the 15.23 to Leeds heading over the viaduct while I was peeing. What a rush!"

Kosi Kalan Railway Station, Platform 2

Kosi Kalan, Uttar Pradesh, India

View: passengers on platform 1 await the arrival of the Agra-Delhi Express

If they have not been already, Ribblehead and the Indian town of Kosi Kalan ought to be twinned. Although at first glance they have absolutely nothing in common, they share a very special bond – united by the fact that they both have a loo from which you can spot trains.

And there are certainly plenty to spot in India. The country's railway system is one of the largest in the world, employing something like 1.6 million people. At the time that the Ribblehead Viaduct was being finished in the 1870s, the railways were already well developed in the British Indian Empire, covering some 14,484 kilometers (9,000 miles) by 1880.

Another railway station said to have a loo with a view is at Fishhoek on the Cape Peninsula in South Africa. During the mating and calving season (July–November), it is said to be possible to see Southern Right Whales while seated. Could it actually get any better?

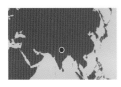

The Maharaja Suite

Sheesh Mahal Palace, Orchha, India

View: standing – the ruins of an Indian kingdom; sitting – a pair of Indian parakeets

Very few indoor toilets have views while seated *and* standing, which makes this find so exciting. Located in the "Maharaja Suite" of a government-run hotel in a former Indian palace, this loo offers a double whammy of pleasure. Here is a throne fit for a king.

The view while standing takes you back to the time of the Bundela kings, who ruled from Orchha between the sixteenth and eighteenth centuries. You stand and picture lavish royal living – camel and elephant houses, ornate gardens, dancing girls, concubines, bathing houses and hunting expeditions into the forest beyond.

While seated you may see a pair of green Indian ring-necked parakeets, which perch on a ledge just outside the window. The chemistry between these lovebirds is electric, making this the perfect place for some loo-based heart-searching.

The Sheesh Mahal sits next to the Jahangir Mahal, a magnificent palace built by the Bundela King Bir Singh Deo to commemorate the visit of the Moghul Emperor Jahangir. It was Jahangir's son, Shah Jahan, who built the famous Taj Mahal in Agra.

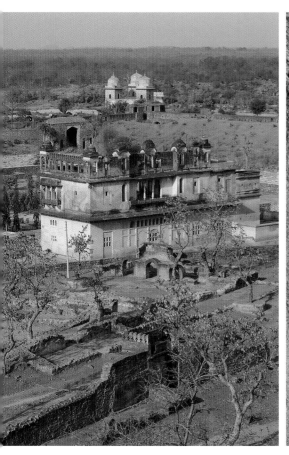

Mount Ruapehu

View: from Hollywood to dunnywood, Mount Ngauruhoe hovers gracefully above the clouds

Unless you are a particularly twisted type of celebrity stalker it is not every day that you see a major film star while visiting a loo. However, this photograph – captured on New Zealand's Mount Ruapehu – proves that it can be done by the general public without breaking the law.

And there she is. Sitting in the distance, her cone elegantly raised above the clouds – Mount Ngauruhoe, a.k.a. the evil Mount Doom in Peter Jackson's celebrated *Lord of the Rings* trilogy.

When not appearing as the home of the "fires of Mordor" in feature films, Mount Ngauruhoe spends its time as an active volcano in Tongariro National Park on the North Island of New Zealand. The park is the oldest National Park in New Zealand.

Eyewitness accounts suggest that there is no view from inside this loo – just a door. However, the general splendor of its location makes it a top loo nonetheless.

Mackinnon Pass

Milford Track, South Island, New Zealand

View: dunnytastic – stand proud and see Clinton Canyon open before your
eyes

Even Shakespeare was into toilets. It has been argued that in *As You Like It* the great man named one of his characters, the melancholy Jaques, after a medieval word for toilet, "jakes." It is good to know that toilet humor was alive and well at the Globe.

And as Jaques famously says in Act 2, Scene 7: "All the world's a stage." Whether Shakespeare meant this line to apply to toilets is doubtful. Nevertheless, this dramatic loo with a view, located on the Milford Track in New Zealand, does have a very theatrical quality.

From backstage, inside the toilet, you catch a glimpse of the view through a window in the door. And then as you exit you make your entrance onto the great platform. The valley opens before you like a pair of curtains. And there it is – the view.

But like a play, the moment does not last for ever. As Jaques says, we all have our exits and our entrances. You take in the view, then take your cue and go on your way.

Jin Mao Building

Grand Hyatt Hotel, Pudong, Shanghai, China

View: from the 56th floor, Shanghai's Oriental Pearl Tower and the Huangpu River

To see truly world-famous sights while using a loo is not always easy. Sometimes it can take both ruthlessness and flexibility. And here is the perfect example. All four of the urinals in this splendid restroom easily offer a view of Shanghai's financial district, Pudong. However, to catch a glimpse of the famous Oriental Pearl Tower takes a little extra commitment to the cause.

First, it is necessary to secure the urinal nearest the window, furthest right. Then, to see the view in all its glory requires a daring "lean back, neck swivel" maneuver. It has been tried and can be done (at your own risk of course).

As well as the spectacular views and location in the super-high eighty-eight-storey Jin Mao Building, the other great thing about these urinals is the divider between the loo and the window, fifty-six floors up, to protect your modesty from the outside world.

Now that is the definition of class.

Mumin Papa Café

View: incredibly, this toilet has been built into an aquarium

Many of the world's most extraordinary toilet experiences lie tantalizingly out of reach. You hear the rumors and read about sightings, but to see them with your own eyes would take years of planning, as well as a degree of luck. Sadly, spotting the Northern Lights, observing whales mating, seeing a rainbow over Machu Picchu and viewing the Earth from space have, thus far, remained elusive.

However, the good news is that in the ladies' loo at the Mumin Papa Café the experience of toileting underwater (while surrounded by a variety of marine animalia) is now perfectly possible.

All too often, women get the short straw when it comes to views from loos. This loo helps to redress the balance. Sit, relax and feel like a mermaid being cradled in the gentle arms of the goddess of the sea.

But can you relax? The loo was recently featured on Japanese television, where the owner explained that a sea turtle living in the aquarium is male and likes to stare at the ladies sitting on the loo!

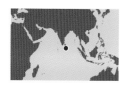

Cloud Forest

Horton Plains National Park, Sri Lanka

View: "tree-mendous" – here is a loo situated in the middle of a tropical forest

Trying to find loos with views is like a sickness – an obsession. You spend your entire life on the lookout. You can't go anywhere without popping into the loo for a quick look. You also spend much of your life feeling disappointed – if you visit somewhere really special or see a beautiful view you just end up wishing that there was a toilet there.

Finding loos with views is a little bit like finding love. Just when you least expect it, completely out of the blue they turn up in the most unlikely places. Like here – hidden deep within a tropical Sri Lankan cloud forest.

Cloud forests are a special type of rainforest, found at relatively high altitudes. You can normally spot a cloud forest by the fact that it is covered in cloud.

The cloud certainly makes it less easy to spot loos with views. But occasionally they find you, appearing out of the mist to rock your world.

Asahi Beer Headquarters, Top Floor Bar

Asakusa, Tokyo, Japan

View: the Sumida River flows through Tokyo on its way to Tokyo Bay

Standing at this top-notch urinal and looking out at modern-day Tokyo – now a huge, densely populated metropolis – it is hard to believe that the city began life as a small fishing village called Edo.

In the late 1500s, at a time when samurai warriors fought on the battlefields of Japan, the head of a powerful clan, Tokugawa Ieyasu, moved his base to Edo. Tokugawa was appointed shogun in AD 1603 and established a dynasty that ruled Japan for over 250 years, while Edo grew into a city of over one million inhabitants.

Officially at least Kyoto remained the capital. But when imperial power was restored to Japan in 1868 (after centuries of merely symbolic leadership) the emperor moved to Edo, which was renamed Tokyo, meaning "eastern capital." It was the start of Japan's modern history.

Just in case it ever comes up in a pub quiz over a pint of beer!

Mequat Mariam

Meket Plateau, Ethiopian Highlands, Ethiopia

View: the "Roof of Africa"

Walking at almost 3,000 meters (9,843 feet) above sea level, the trek takes you across the Meket Plateau to a spectacular escarpment and your home for the night - the thatched *tukuls* of Mequat Mariam. And (would you believe it?) one of them – the open-fronted *tukul* nearest the camera – happens to house one of the finest loos with a view in all of Africa.

Your hosts at Mequat Mariam work in partnership with an organization called "Tourism in Ethiopia for Sustainable Future Alternatives" (TESFA), a non-profit-making NGO, which helps local communities in the Ethiopian Highlands build services for tourists. Four villages now host tourists on the Meket Plateau and more are developing facilities, including, of course, loos with views.

Sitting in this magnificent *tukul*, watching birds soaring in the skies above and knowing that your business is helping communities to develop in one of the world's poorest countries offers a sense of well-being that is not easy to find in the world today. This is the perfect way to start or end your day. This is the perfect way to see the world.

INTERM

EISSION

a.k.a. toilet break

Exciting sneak preview of nominees for the forthcoming (fictional)

Loo View Awards

(LAVs)

Best view
while standing

W.C

Desert WC, Close to the Ksar Ghilane Oasis, Sahara Desert, Tunisia

Best view while seated in an outdoor setting

"The Chateau," Wolwedans Lodge, NamibRand Nature Reserve, Namibia

Best view
while entering
or exiting

Santa Cruz Trek, Bolivia

Best view
of a loo

Croagh Patrick, County Mayo, Ireland

Felix Bar

Peninsula Hotel, Kowloon, Hong Kong

View: classic loo-based tourism – see Hong Kong Harbor and Island from the ladies' restroom

It was a tough call deciding whether to feature the ladies' or the gents' at the Felix. While the men's is well known for its urinal views of Kowloon (giving it a much higher "view from the actual loo" rating), the fact that ladies can powder their noses while looking at one of the world's most iconic views makes this a female victory.

Hong Kong Harbor is also known as Victoria Harbor – after Her Royal Highness, who was on the throne when Britain took control of Hong Kong in the 1840s. Also named after Queen Victoria are Lake Victoria in East Africa, Victoria Falls, the Victoria sponge cake and Victoria Park, home of Hartlepool United Football Club.

This is not the only Hong Kong-based loo to appear in a book. Rumor has it that a loo with a view at the former premises of the Foreign Correspondents' Club of Hong Kong, Sutherland House, was featured in the John le Carré spy thriller *The Honorable Schoolboy.*

Kalamu Tented Camp

The Banks of the South Luangwa River, Zambia

View: wallowing hippopotami

We have seen that loos with views allow us to sightsee from the toilet. However, another popular tourist pursuit, also perfectly possible from loos, is big-game spotting. The safari parks of Africa are a gold mine for loos with views. Elephant, hippo, crocodile – numerous sightings have been recorded. Put down the morning paper – this is the only way to start the day.

To see all of the "big five" (lion, elephant, buffalo, rhino and leopard) or to see a kill from the loo is incredibly rare, incredibly difficult and takes incredible dedication – or incredible bowel trouble.

But there is plenty to contemplate as you wait: the great "circle of life," as discussed in Disney's *The Lion King*; how "survival of the fittest" theories became ingrained into Fascist ideas about the survival of nations with catastrophic effects; or the thought that we look at animals going to the loo all the time and think nothing of it, but looking at animals while we go to the loo somehow feels a bit surreal!

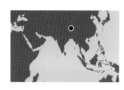

Samye Monastery

Shannan, Tibet

View: from this communal, triple toilet (sadly only two loos are in view here), a shrine at the oldest monastery in Tibet

You could devote an entire book to communal toileting. From Roman soldiers to farmers in the Australian outback to Buddhist monks, going "en masse" is not only a part of human history, it is also common practice in a number of cultures today.

Even in Britain, a country known for its prudish sensibilities, it was not so long ago that children grew up on two-seater toilets in their back gardens. Rare "three-seaters" have even been discovered.

Collective toileting, while perhaps initially off-putting, is good for the soul – solid, character-building stuff. What conversations must have been had and what relationships must have been forged. Has there ever been a marriage proposal?

Rising divorce rates, a breakdown in family values and a lack of community are all big issues in the modern world. But perhaps the answer is staring us right in the face? Perhaps the answer is communal toilets?

Galata Tower

Galata, Istanbul, Turkey

View: intercontinental toileting – from Europe into Asia, while seated

There are only a handful of places on Earth where it is possible to sit on a loo and see into another continent. With views across the Bosporus Strait into Asia, this fine throne, located high in Istanbul's Galata Tower, is one of them. The window is made of frosted glass, but opens to create a quite magnificent loo with a view. "Breezy but breathtaking," commented one American tourist.

Throughout its history, Istanbul has been a place of great strategic and commercial importance – the center of empires. For centuries the city was known as Constantinople after the Roman Emperor Constantine, who declared it the capital of the Roman Empire in the fourth century.

The Galata Tower was built in 1348. In the seventeenth century, when Istanbul was under Ottoman control, it is said that an early aviator called Hezarfen Ahmet Çelebi jumped from the top of the tower and glided with artificial wings across the Bosporus. Had this toilet existed at the time, he may have wished to use it before making his historic leap.

St Helen's Oratory

Upstairs Bathroom, Cape Cottage, Cornwall, United Kingdom

View: the site of an ancient Christian chapel and wild Atlantic coastline

And so here is where the journey began – a freckly-faced, floppy-haired young lad sits on a loo and sees a view. Cows were grazing, waves were crashing against the rocks and the sun was shining. What a moment and what a loo.

The chapel, known as St Helen's Oratory, may date back to around the fifth century. It is certainly likely to have been built after Emperor Constantine's famous conversion in AD 312, which transformed Christianity into an official religion within the Roman Empire. Constantine's conversion changed the course of human history – little did he know that centuries later it would also create this fantastic loo view.

Well-placed windows in bathrooms can take us to places we never dreamed we would go and into worlds that we never thought we would visit. Everyone should have access to a loo with a view – they change lives.

Incredibly, a family in the west of England are currently considering moving their toilet three feet to the right to give it a view of the largest church cockerel in Europe! Now that's the spirit.

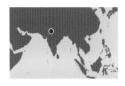

Just outside
Thiksey Buddhist Monastery

Leh, Ladakh, India

View: serene scene, high in the Himalayas while standing

From: Sourav Basu

To: loos@looswithviews.com

Dear Luke,

Congratulations on the successful publication of your new book. The moment I read about it in today's newspaper, I decided to write to you. I will wait for your book to arrive in local book store here in Bangalore, India.

I am sending you a photo taken by me and would be extremely happy if it makes a place in the next edition of your book.

The photo is taken at a peaceful and serene loo located just outside the Thiksey Buddhist Monastery in Leh, Ladakh, India.

Best Regards,

Sourav Basu

Literally the best day of my life.

Beachside Cabana

Mazunte Beach, Mexico

View: Armageddon?

As the Hollywood blockbuster *2012* makes clear, the calendar of the ancient Mayans only runs until the year 2012 when, according to legend, human civilization will be wiped out.

However, what the film doesn't discuss is that the world will end, or so the story I heard goes anyway, when a giant comet hits earth at the "Punta Cometa" (Comet Point), Mazunte Beach, Mexico – i.e. here!

What's more, the film neglects to mention that Comet Point (center frame with tuft sticking up) is visible from this toilet! I'm particularly hurt they left that out. Come 2012 this may well be the best seat in the house – albeit potentially a dangerous one.

By an extraordinary twist of fate Rhiannon May Jones, the loo hunter/holiday maker who unearthed this exciting gem, was traveling with someone whose father collects interesting and historical toilet rolls – the study of which is called cloacopapyrology.

As well as a view of the very spot at which human life on Planet Earth might end, it is also thought possible to see whales and manta rays while seated.

Airship

Floating above California, United States

View: magical – constantly changing before your eyes

Planes, trains, boats, bicycles and airships – toilets on the move are an exciting addition to the "loos with views" family. They offer a unique, often uplifting, travel experience – and no two visits are ever the same.

I have been told about several, including the Trans Siberian Express; first class on several airlines; the Waverley paddle steamer; and a urinal view on the ferry from Portsmouth to the Isle of Wight from which it may be possible to see Osborne House, Queen Victoria's family getaway.

Incredibly, I have also heard tell of ships where the captain's seat doubles as a toilet so that he/she can continue to steer while attending nature's call. I'm not sure that I'd want to eat at that captain's table.

Airship Ventures offer flights to tourists in LA and San Francisco. Potential sightings from their loo include the Hollywood Sign and the Golden Gate Bridge. It may also be possible to see Alcatraz Island in San Francisco Bay – in which case users could look out for the loo in the guard's tower (p32). Now there's an exciting thought.

Of course I haven't found any toilets on bicycles, but I live in hope.

Table Mountain

Upstairs toilet (the one furthest left), Ashanti Lodge, Cape Town, South Africa

View: the mighty Table Mountain

Of all the loos with views in the world, this might well be the most talked about. I have heard of it from at least FOUR separate sources – more than any other loo on the planet.

And it's easy to see why it's so memorable. As well as the magnificent view across the rooftops to Table Mountain, the attention to detail here is staggering:

1. The toilet was moved to allow users to see the view through the window clearly while seated.

2. There's a lovely mosaic on the toilet wall, depicting the mountain and the cable car that takes you to the top.

3. Perhaps most exciting, binoculars are provided (on a chain by the window) to allow users to make the most of this unique opportunity.

Table Mountain is one of the most iconic sights in South Africa. It is characterized by a three-kilometer-long level plateau and offers incredible views, including Robben Island, where Nelson Mandela was famously imprisoned.

"Pissoir Superstar"

Marisco Tavern, Lundy Island, United Kingdom

View: out to sea, with the mainland in the distance

I didn't dare dream it possible. When I visited the Station Inn, Ribblehead, and marveled at the sight of trains crossing a magnificent twenty-four-arch viaduct (p62), I remember thinking that this had to be Britain's finest view from a pub urinal – undisputed.

But now there's a rival to the crown – a new urinal in town.

These two need to get into a ring and sort this thing out. Or perhaps there should be a new TV show to find Britain's best pub urinal and they could go head-to-head for the public vote in the live final? Possible titles: *Pissoir Superstar*, *Stand and Deliver* or *I'm a Urinal, Get in Front of Me*.

This is an open-air, outdoor facility. Users stand before the white wall (pictured in foreground) with a gutter for drainage. Note the water pipe for added proof that this is a urinal.

Owned by The National Trust, Lundy Island lies nineteen kilometers (12 miles) off the coast of north Devon, where the Bristol Channel meets the Atlantic. As well as beautiful loo-views, it offers a variety of activities, including walking and bird-watching.

Cape Cornwall Car Park

View: man with prominent nose in a bath?

Sadly, this facility has no view from inside (unless you're into soap dispensers). However, with the fantastic Brisons rocks as a backdrop, it arguably boasts the best view while entering/exiting a toilet block in Britain.

The Brisons lie almost two kilometers (1.24 miles) out to sea. Every year, intrepid swimmers are taken out in fishing boats for the daring "Brisons Swim" back to shore. It is likely that the rocks were once used as a prison, as the Cornish for prison is brison. Today the rocks are an important breeding ground for sea birds.

The likeness to a man lying in the bath certainly cannot be denied. Many even say that it's Le Général himself – the great French leader Charles de Gaulle – on account of the protruding proboscis.

There is also an excellent seasonal snack van in the car park – a "brew with a view?"

As well as his association with the Brisons, the main airport in Paris is also named after Charles de Gaulle.

Other toilet blocks in car parks with notable views when exiting include the Croagh Patrick car park facility in County Mayo, Ireland (p20).

[108]

Grand Canyon

Salt Creek Camp, Tonto Trail, Grand Canyon NP, Arizona, United States

View: stunning red rock formations

"Ahhh, Lucas old boy ... just chatting to someone at church – they remember a double-seater with a view across the Grand Canyon ... used it about twenty years ago ... I'll leave it with you ..." (My father, December 2008)

Goodness knows I tried. But I've been unable to track down this phenomenal sounding toilet. Dad, I've let you down.

However, I have found one of its neighbors. And, boy, what a toilet it is! Although the view while seated remains a mystery to me, standing users look out across the Grand Canyon National Park to the "Tower of Set" – the beautiful rock formation on the horizon.

Many of the rocks in this area of the park have Egyptian names. Conspiracy theories abound and some believe there's a more direct link to Ancient Egypt in the canyon with artifacts rumored to have been discovered within a secret network of caves, which are off-limits to the public.

Some toilets in the park are flown in and out, suspended under helicopters. Now there's a good idea for a new extreme sport.

Mount Elbrus

The "Barrels" mountain huts, Caucasus, Russia

View: breathtaking scenery while squatting in the shadow of Elbrus

I searched long and hard to find a loo-view of the scene of a Greek myth. Attempts at Theseus and the Minotaur, The Twelve Labours of Heracles and Icarus and Daedalus sadly proved fruitless. So you can imagine how thrilled I was to learn that Mount Elbrus, the home of no less than TWO loo-views, is a key player in the story of Prometheus. Eureka!

Prometheus is said to have stolen fire from the Gods. As a punishment, Zeus banishes him to Elbrus, where he is chained to a rock and has his liver eaten by an eagle every day – only for it to grow back every night and be eaten again the following day.

At least the view was scenic for poor Prometheus, although can you really appreciate anything when your liver is being repeatedly eaten by an eagle?

Mount Elbrus is the highest mountain in Europe at 18,510 feet (5,642 meters), although some say that Elbrus is in Asia and that the distinction belongs to Mont Blanc at 15,781 feet (4,810 meters).
I don't believe it – mainly because I haven't found any loo-views of Mont Blanc.

Canterbury Cathedral

Ladies Loo, Upstairs in Deeson's British Restaurant,
Canterbury, Kent, United Kingdom

View: the spiritual home of the Church of England and the worldwide
Anglican Communion, as you sit

After writing *A Loo with a View*, my friend Tim Court and
I brainstormed ideas for further projects based around
the same theme. They included: a toilet-based snooker/
pool tournament called A Loo with a Cue™; a toilet-based
speed-dating business – brand name A Loo with a Woo™;
and a detective novel/movie called A Loo with a Clue. There
was even A Loo with Déjà-vu, which, in the spirit of Alan
Partridge's *A Partridge Amongst the Pigeons* idea, was "just
a title."

Sadly, none of our ideas seems to have materialized. That
is, until now. Ladies and gentlemen, I am proud to present
A Loo with a Pew (toilets with views of churches).

Fear not. Despite frosted glass on the lower window, the cathedral is visible through the
upper while seated – and also looks heavenly when flood-lit at night.

Canterbury Cathedral dates from AD 597, when St Augustine, sent by the Pope as a
missionary, established his seat (a.k.a. cathedral) in Canterbury. The cathedral is symbolic
of the tension between religion and state – in 1170, Archbishop Thomas Beckett was
famously murdered inside by four knights of King Henry II.

BT Tower

Heights Bar, St Georges Hotel, Langham Place, London

View: one of two major communications towers now known to be visible

from urinals

As I dried my hands and walked towards the elevator, to descend from the Jin Mao Building back to the streets of Shanghai, I wondered with sadness whether this might just be the last time I ever saw a major communications tower from a urinal (p72).

Imagine my delight, then, when news reached me that right in the heart of London – under my very nose – sat a urinal with a view of the iconic BT Tower. The dream lives on.

BT was also excited to hear of the find: "This really is tremendous news," said a spokesman.

The BT Tower has been part of the London skyline since the 1960s and was officially opened to the public in May 1966 by Tony Benn, MP and Sir Billy Butlin, whose leisure company (Butlins) operated a revolving restaurant at the top.

Also visible from the loo (in the distance with a 90-degree neck twist) is St Paul's Cathedral, as you look out across Soho and Bloomsbury towards the river (more content for A Loo with a Pew – damn, it's going to be good).

As well as the view, this loo also boasts a working shoe-polishing machine.

[116]

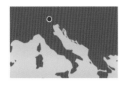

Refuge de Lagazuoi

Dolomites Mountains, Italy

View: through the window from the peak of Mount Lagazuoi

(with radiator for added comfort)

Of all the various genres of "loo-view," my favorite is "historical." We spend an awful lot of our lives locked in bathrooms and, once in a while, it's refreshing to walk into a toilet and be transported back into history.

And here, located at a splendid mountain inn high in the Dolomites, is a classic example. As you sit gazing out of the window it's incredible to think that beneath you, within the bowels of the mountain, are tunnels (now an open-air museum) dating back to the First World War.

They were dug by the Austro-Hungarian and Italian armies, as they waged a ferocious war in the Dolomites. Both armies set up bases inside the mountain, attempting to destroy the other with dynamite.

I have taken the liberty of "tagging" the photo, to show just how impressive the location of this loo is.

Other loos associated with wartime tunnels include one at Dover Castle in the UK (p36). Both sets of tunnels are open to the public. Lagazuoi can be reached on foot or by cable car/chair lift.

Just Below the Peak of Mount Rysy

Mountain Chalet Toilet, High Tatra Mountains, Slovakia

View: multi-faceted – spectacular while waiting, out through a

heart-shaped hole and the loo is a view in itself

It wouldn't be an exaggeration to describe this toilet as a cocoon of joy. Perched high in the High Tatra Mountains, here is a loo that is high on life. If it ordered an alcoholic drink, it'd be a "Grin and Tonic"!!!!! Raucous!!!!!

Painted decorations include: a smiling sun, a cute bird, a handsome snail, floating balloons and a cheeky toadstool with its tongue sticking out.

And if that wasn't enough, the inside is also decorated and features a heart-shaped hole – no doubt for ventilation, as well as a reminder for us all to view the world with joy and love in our hearts.

The popular Rysy Mountain sits on the border between Poland and Slovakia and is Poland's highest peak.

There used to be a border crossing on the summit. However, this was shut down in 2007, when a border cooperation scheme was adopted between the two countries.

A Loo Set Free

Mountain Restaurant, High Above Zermatt, Switzerland

View: captured from the urinal, the Matterhorn as seen through broken frosted glass

For anyone trying to find loos with great views, the sight of frosted glass is a constant thorn in the dream, leading to countless "what ifs" and "if onlys."

And so I was heartened to see this astonishing photograph. A loo finds its view – a loo is set free – and with it, gone is the heartache of countless frost-induced disappointments.

But is there something bigger going on here? Could this have been a calculated act? Is there a global movement of undercover activists out there, dedicated to the eradication of frosted glass in public toilets?

It might sound ridiculous, but I've done some investigating and can reveal that the domain name "frost-sucks.org" is unavailable. The plot thickens?

No it doesn't. I totally made that up.

The author does not encourage vandalism of any kind.

"Cock-a-Doodle-Loo"

View: enormous gold plated church cockerel

Massive news from Cock View Manor! If preliminary plans are approved, this loo will soon be turned 180 degrees to face a new floor-to-ceiling window made entirely of one-way glass. What's more, the uplifting sound of male voice choirs will be piped into the bathroom on a continuous loop. What a truly exciting experience it will be, like being serenaded from heaven.

But for the time being, it still remains a pretty good loo-view. It doesn't get much better than seeing Europe's largest church cockerel (as claimed by local residents) from a toilet. Measuring in at 1.8 meters by 1.5 meters (5.9 by 4.92 feet), the whopping bird has sat proud on top of the village church for around 200 years. It must have seen a thing or two in its time.

Seeing the cockerel while using the loo currently requires users (male) to stand to the right, with knees bent and neck strained in order to line up with the only available gap in the tree. It certainly isn't easy, but you do get to see the (reputed) largest church cockerel in Europe from a toilet.

*Address changed to protect identity of owners

Loos 7 & 11

Mount Baker, Washington, United States

View: either a sensational view from the mountain or your climbing buddy's back

In 1792, a British ship commanded by explorer George Vancouver was mapping the Pacific Northwest Coast of America. As the ship sat anchored in Dungeness Bay, 3rd Lieutenant Joseph Baker spotted a rather impressive mountain. Mount Baker was born.

By an extraordinary twist of fate, the gentleman who captured this fantastic image on Mount Baker recalls seeing the "twinkling lights of the city of Vancouver" (named after Baker's commander, of course) from a toilet on the mountain.

Sensational historical toileting!

The numbers on the loos reveal that Mount Baker is home to at least eleven toilets – no doubt all with views. To use them all in one day would be challenging on so many levels.

Mount Baker had been known to the indigenous population for centuries. The Spanish also "discovered" it in 1790.

The position of the seat hinges proves that the toilets face the same way. Assuming both are occupied simultaneously, I'm undecided which I'd be more comfortable using!

Melbourne Cricket Ground

35th Floor, Sofitel, Melbourne, Australia

View: the famous MCG (easily seen from sinks – neck twist required from urinals)

Mentioned in guide books and famous throughout Melbourne, this loo has become a tourist stop in its own right. But a visit is also a great way to see the city – visible from it is the State Parliament, the Treasury and, perhaps most exciting, the Melbourne Cricket Ground, also the symbolic home of Australian Rules football.

Funnily enough, I was informed by a fan of the Aussie Rules team the "London Swans" (she was also a member of the sister netball team, the "Swanettes") that the Ladies has a similarly impressive view from the cubicle nearest the window. She suspected that I was using the loo-book story as an elaborate ruse and that I was actually a spy from local rivals the "West London Wildcats." Cover maintained...

Other major grounds known to be visible from toilets are:

1. Lords Cricket Ground (p42)

2. PCN Park, home of the Pittsburgh Pirates (overleaf)

I have also heard of a loo inside the MCG with a view of the pitch, but sadly this remains unconfirmed, for now.

Room 1023

Renaissance Hotel, Pittsburgh, Pennsylvania, United States

View: a dream come true – live Major League Baseball, while seated

Following the release of the 1994 hit movie *Four Weddings and a Funeral*, demand for the "Elizabeth I Four Poster Suite" at The Crown in Amersham – the location of Hugh Grant and Andie McDowell's first love scene – is said to have sky-rocketed.

The same is bound to happen here. From now on, 1023 is sure to be the hottest room in town.

And what a view it is – across the Allegheny River into the home of the Pittsburgh Pirates. It's even possible to see the home plate and all four bases – making the view particularly special on game days.

Also visible is the Roberto Clemente Bridge, named after the former Pirates' right fielder, who was tragically killed in a plane crash on New Year's Eve, 1972, trying to deliver aid to Nicaragua following an earthquake.

It is only natural to compare this loo to the toilet with a view of the MCG (see previous entry). Unlike Melbourne, it offers a view inside of the stadium (1–0). However, it requires users to rent a room (1–1). It is swings and roundabouts in the loo-view game.

Bucket Race

Conconully Outhouse Races, Washington, United States

View: inside of bucket

With hearts pumping they run – pushing a purpose-built, three-sided wooden outhouse on skis through the snow with buckets on their heads. A third team member bravely sits inside, shouting directions over the deafening noise of the crowd. This is the Conconully Bucket Race. This is the greatest race on earth.

There has been outhouse racing at Conconully for at least a quarter of a century. Outhouses are raced head-to-head down the main street in a number of divisions (not all races involve buckets). According to the rules of competition, all outhouses must be equipped with a toilet seat and toilet roll on a hanger and all riders must wear helmets.

Outhouse racing is alive and well in the United States. There are a number of different races in a number of different states – some on skis, some on wheels.

Although not technically "real" toilets, they offer a unique adrenalin-filled loo-view experience for the rider and so are worthy of inclusion.

Outhouse racing is yet to catch on in Britain – although I have been lucky enough to witness a number of "duck races" down village streams, using plastic ducks.

Baños Públicos in Los Flamencos

Laguna Miñique, Los Flamencos National Reserve, Atacama Desert, Chile

View: the stunning Miñique Lagoon and Miñique Volcano

In 2009, a couple from London embarked on an epic journey together, vowing before they left to find a loo with a view.

Their first challenge was to cycle across America – an epic (4,163-mile) 6,700-kilometer road trip. They "thought of me" in every toilet they entered. But nothing.

Next stop was South America, where they were on the verge of tracking down a loo with a view in Los Glaciares National Park, Argentina, before being thwarted at the last minute by a landslide.

Just days before they were due to return home, "empty-handed," it happened. Some things are just meant to be.

This loo symbolizes the spirit of adventure and dedication to the cause that has made this book possible.

The loo offers magical views while exiting. It may also offer a view through the door while seated (as pictured). However, this requires the door to be left open (risky if there's a line) and for users to lean forward with a twist neck – not the most dignified maneuver, but technically possible.

How cute is the ventilation chimney?!

Scilly Isles

Dolphin House, Tresco, Isles of Scilly, United Kingdom

View: across to Old Grimsby Quay and Islands beyond

The scene of a blissful family holiday, I had long dreamed of seeing a "loo with a view" on the Isles of Scilly. There were exciting rumors of three-sided huts looking out to sea, but the island's loo-views remained tantalizingly out of reach.

Finally, it happened – and the wait was certainly worth it.

The "Scillies" sit in the Atlantic Ocean, some 45 kilometers off Lands End – the most westerly point in Britain. Tresco is one of five inhabited islands in the archipelago. Thanks to a sub-tropical climate, the famous Abbey Gardens are able to thrive on the island, filled with exotic plants from around the world.

The Scillies are known to have the smallest soccer league in the world – one pitch and two clubs, who are said to play each other seventeen times every season, competing for two cups as well as the league title.

You will be pleased to know that this view is also visible from the bath.

On a clear day the Scillies are visible from Cape Cornwall (p120). Thanks to the Tresco Estate, who own and rent Dolphin House as a holiday cottage.

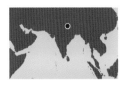

Nomadic Loo Tent

Annapurna Foothills, Himalayas, Nepal

View: great start to the day – captured just after dawn, the Annapurna range including sacred Machapuchare

Nomadic in nature, loo tents offer a constantly changing view. Like the "Littlest Hobo," of TV dog fame, they "keep on moving on," don't like to be tied down (metaphorically at least) and bring relief to those they meet.

Although it has no view from inside, this tent must have been pitched in some pretty exciting places in its time. And none more so than here – pegged down at 1,600 meters (5,249 feet) above sea level in the foothills of the Annapurna Range in the Himalayas.

Machapuchare is pictured directly above the tent. Also known as Fish-tail Mountain on account of its double summit (which looks a bit like a fish-tail) the mountain is now closed to climbers, as it's regarded as sacred to the Hindu god Shiva. A British expedition got close to the top in 1957. However, they stopped just shy because they had promised not to set foot on the summit.

You could produce a whole book, or even feature-length documentary, about the life and times of a loo tent – possible title: In Search of the Perfect Pitch. Surely a winner?

MAX

View: a train that looks like an animal?

Tokyo is a veritable hotbed for urinal views. A city of limited space, where things are built upwards, it offers ideal conditions for spectacular toileting.

But of all the urinals in all of Tokyo, this has the potential to deliver something truly extraordinary. With a clear view of the railway line near Tokyo Station, it might just be possible to stand before it and see my favorite bullet train – the E4 Series "MAX" (Multi Amenity express).

It's a double-decker and, of course, travels at lightning speed (max 240km/h; 149 m./h). But, best of all, it looks a bit like an animal. I think a rampaging bison (others say carp fish). I have heard stories of tourists arriving in Tokyo and heading straight to the station, just to see it. This is the way trains ought to be – as exciting as it must have felt when the first steam locomotives were built in the nineteenth century.

I have deliberately not researched whether the "MAX" travels on this particular line. I am not sure I could handle it if not.

Hiroshima Peace Memorial Park

Hiroshima, Honshū, Japan

View: the world famous Hiroshima Peace Memorial, or "A-Dome"

It was once the Hiroshima Industrial Promotions Hall. Today it's a World Heritage site and one of the world's most iconic structures. The A-Dome stands as a memorial to those killed by the atomic bomb of 6 August 1945. Now it promotes peace.

The bomb detonated 580 meters (1,903 feet) above ground and just 150 meters (492 feet) away from the Dome – causing instant and unparalleled death and destruction to the city. An estimated 140,000 were killed, many after the initial explosion as a result of radiation poisoning, and some 70 percent of Hiroshima's buildings were destroyed.

Somehow the Dome stayed standing. Hiroshima was rebuilt around it and today the Dome is a constant reminder of the devastating cost of nuclear war.

Hiroshima became a "peace memorial city" and, as such, every time a country authorizes the detonation of a nuclear device, the Mayor of Hiroshima writes to its leader in protest.

Japan surrendered shortly after the bombings of Hiroshima and of Nagasaki, three days later. Some argue that the bombs were justified as they brought the war to a speedy end, ultimately resulting in fewer deaths than if Japan had continued to fight on.

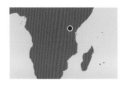

Kilimanjaro

Karanga Valley, Mount Kilimanjaro, Tanzania

View: amazing – it's the highest point in Africa

Progress in the "Seven Summits" loo-view challenge (the seven summits are the highest peaks in each of the seven continents):

Africa, Kilimanjaro ✓

Antarctica, Vinson Massif
Rumors of an ice toilet, accessible by plane, at base camp with view of the peak
(unconfirmed)

Australasia, Kosciuszko
Have read that a toilet has been built on the peak
(unconfirmed)

Asia, Everest ✓
At the Tengboche Monastery, Nepal (p24)

Europe, Elbrus ✓ ✓
Double check!
(p50 and p106)

North America, McKinley ✓
Tentative check. Loo at 4,328 meters (14,200 feet). View while sitting is of Mount Foraker. However, view while standing is unknown and may include the peak
(p60)

South America, Aconcagua
Sadly, no check.

4/7 (albeit with one tentative check).

Oh geez – I think I might know too much about toilets.

To reach all seven summits is a major achievement in mountaineering. Likewise, visiting a loo with a view of each peak would be considered a major achievement in toilet hunting.

Shower

Backpacker Hostel, Cusco, Peru

View: the historic capital of the Incan Empire as you exfoliate

From: Gabrielle Carter

To: Luke Barclay

Cc: Mel

Subject: Ducha with a Viewsha?

Dear Luke,

Don't suppose you're at all interested in views from showers are you? My fiancé once peed in one, if that helps?

Hope to hear from you soon.

Best wishes,

Gabz

A view from a shower!? Talk about pushing the boundaries. What's next? Bidets?

I have also heard tell of a shower in Uganda with a view of the source of the Nile – the greatest hair wash on Earth?

Cusco is a World Heritage City and the historical capital of Peru. It was once the center of the Inca Empire, which spanned much of western South America in the fifteenth and sixteenth centuries, before the arrival of the Spanish conquistadors.

Mountain Hut

High above Mayrhofen, Tirol, Austria

View: voyeuristic goat

List of reported animal sightings from loos:

1. African elephants, crossing river, Zambia (p70)
2. Hippopotami, wallowing in river, Zambia (p74)
3. Crocodile, lurking in river, Zambia (anecdotal, 2 sources)
4. Urban fox cubs, frolicking on garden lawn, London (anecdotal)
5. Green Indian ring-necked parakeets, perching, India (p66)
6. Southern right whales, mating, South Africa (anecdotal)
7. Marmots, looking cute, United States (anecdotal, 2 sources)
8. Black Noddy terns, mating and rearing young in nests, Great Barrier Reef (p40)
9. Goat, staring, Austria (this page)

This might be the closest we have come to finding a loo-view of the scene of a famous masterpiece, with Marc Chagall often including goats in his paintings.
For example, the "violin-playing goat" discussed in the movie *Notting Hill*.

Theories abound as to the significance of goats for Chagall. One is that he was referring to the Jewish Day of Atonement, when a goat was sent out into the wilderness to atone for man's sins.

Or maybe he just liked goats?

Halfway Guesthouse

Tiger Leaping Gorge, Yunnan Province, China

View: gaze across the gorge while squatting with the Yangtze River rushing below

While it remains possible that Take That's Gary Barlow has seen the loos featured on Kilimanjaro, we know for SURE that a television legend has visited these. Broadcast in 2004, Michael Palin traveled through Tiger Leaping Gorge for his *Himalayas* series which aired in Britain – stopping at the Halfway Guesthouse and passing comment on the phenomenal loo-view.

And what a view it is. To enjoy it for a prolonged period certainly requires strong legs. But I think it's worth training for in advance. This is an extraordinary canyon – 15 kilometers (9.3 miles) long with sheer 2,000 meter (6,562 feet) cliffs. Legend has it that a tiger once leapt across the river to evade a hunter, which is how the gorge gets its name.

The loo is advertised on rocks on the trail: "24 hour hot shower, delicious pancake, home-made apple pie and scenic toilet view." What a combination.

Measuring in at just shy of 6,500 kilometers (4,039 miles), the Yangtze River is the third longest in the world, behind the Nile and the Amazon.

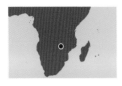

Banks of the Zambezi

Old Mondoro Bush Camp, Lower Zambezi National Park, Zambia

View: "trunk-tastic!" Best see at "tusk?"

With a clear sight of the Zambezi while seated or from the sinks, today this loo is a great place for toilet-based game spotting – elephant, hippo and croc are all said to have been seen from it.

However, had the loo existed in the nineteenth century, users might also have seen Dr. Livingstone as he traveled down the river on his way to discovering Victoria Falls.

In fact, given that there's also a loo on Livingstone Island with a view of the falls (p34), one could technically now journey in the great man's footsteps, stopping at loos along the way.

Windmill Village

Zaanse Schans, Zaandam, Netherlands

View: windmills

The banks of the River Zaan were once teeming with activity. This was the heartland of early-industrial Holland – many hundreds of mills, harnessing the natural power of the wind to produce everything from corn to cloth to cocoa.

Today, Zaanse Schans – an open-air museum and conservation area – is one of Holland's top tourist destinations. As well as windmills, historic shipyards and clog-making demos, sights include this traditional toilet, which overhangs the river – taking you back to life before the flush.

Sanitation has moved on in modern-day Holland. But today, in many parts of the world, communities don't have access to even this basic kind of toilet facility. Some 2.5 billion people are said to live without access to adequate sanitation, leading to unnecessary disease and death.

Charities such as the UK-based Pump Aid are working towards breaking the toilet taboo and improving this dire situation. See www.pumpaid.org for more information about their work.

This view rivals "goat from urinal" for the loo-view which most resembles a famous work of art. It's reminiscent of a number of paintings by French artist Claude Monet, including his *Windmills near Zaandam*.

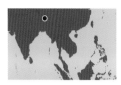

Monks En Masse

Buddhist Monastery, Tibet

View: a rare find – many monks can utilize simultaneously

Ten outdoor toilets, lined up in a row at a monastery in Tibet.
One word ...
AWESOME.

Other notable examples of "communal toileting" include:

1. The loos of the Roman legionaries: ruins can be seen at Ephesus in Turkey, Sabratha and Leptis Magna in Libya, and Hadrian's Wall (particularly at Housesteads Fort) in Northumbria, UK.

2. A "three-holer" at Kelmscott Manor, Gloucestershire, UK, the country home of the nineteenth-century artist, poet and socialist William Morris. The house is open to the public, but sadly you're not allowed to use the loo.

3. Incredibly, King Louis XIV of France is said to have announced his betrothal from his commode – every girl's dream? Both he and Louis XIII gave audience while "seated," with Louis XIII said to have had a commode built into his throne.

It's not surprising that a number of the communal toilets found in this search have been located at Buddhist monasteries or temples, as Buddhism is a religion that encourages us to live without ego.

Antarctica

Portable Latrine, Hovgaard Island

View: in 24-hour daylight, the silent magnificent beauty of the Antarctic

OCCUPIED

It feels inappropriate to interrupt the unique and personal experience of sitting alone, looking out at the edge of Earth's last untouched wilderness.

But I will anyway.

This toilet has been described as "the eighth wonder of the world." However, of the original seven wonders of the ancient world it may be possible to see the only surviving member, the Great Pyramid at Giza, from a toilet. I received news from an air-hostess that first-class passengers (who often have windows in their toilets) can potentially enjoy a loo-view of the pyramids shortly before landing at Cairo. My loo spies are everywhere!

However, she did point out that the "fasten seat belt" sign might well be on by this stage, making such an endeavor dangerous and probably illegal.

Valle Gran Rey

Mirador César Manrique, La Gomera, Canary Islands

View: "look-out" over the Valle Gran Rey

Despite the absence of a "loo" picture to prove that this is a bona fide loo-view, I have it on good authority that both the Ladies and Gents offer the same spectacular view across the Valle Gran Rey on the island of La Gomera.

However, I am aware that my reputation as a finder of loo-views is on the line here, so I can confirm that I have discovered a second source. The *Guardian* newspaper, no less: "This place would win 'the world's best view from a lavatory award' hands down," wrote Jonathan Lee in 2005.

That's good enough for me, although I hope to have demonstrated that there's some pretty stiff competition out there for such an award.

I am aware that Jonathan Lee is male, so this doesn't necessarily confirm the view from the Ladies, but as Austin Powers once said: "throw me a frickin' bone here."

Isla del Sol

Lake Titicaca, Copacabana, Peru

View: through holes in door, or with door open, gaze in awe across
Lake Titicaca to Bolivia

From: Luke Barclay

To: Gabrielle Carter

Cc: Mel

Subject: Loo Mission

Don't suppose you guys are going anywhere near
Copacabana are you? There have been sightings...

Details to follow, should you choose to accept this daring
mission...

Kind regards,

Luke

And so it was that with no money to stay on the island and their ride back to the mainland departing in minutes, Gabz and Mel continued their desperate search of the Isla del Sol. "Look – Inca ruins!" said Mel, as they ran. "Are they a toilet Mel!? NOT interested ..." replied Gabz. They were about to throw in the towel when they saw it. But elation turned to despair – the door was padlocked! A group of travelers practicing "laughter yoga" (or maybe they were laughing at Gabz and Mel) offered to go and get the keys. But there was no time. This was snatch and grab – loo hunting on the edge.

The beautiful Isla del Sol is accessible from Copacabana and is famous for Inca ruins.

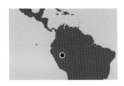

Inca Trail

Andes, Peru

View: not Machu Picchu

When I set out on my quest to find the world's best loos with views, I penned a list of views that I wanted to find. It included "Mount Everest, preferably peak," "large game e.g. elephant," "the northern lights," "the earth from space" and "the scene of a Constable painting." Happily, many have now been found, photographed and crossed off. Some, however, remain elusive.

And none more so than "a loo with a view" of the "lost city" of Machu Picchu. But at least we're getting closer and are on the Inca Trail – the ancient path to Machu Picchu, which winds its way to the city via mountain passes, cloud forests and Inca ruins.

Although we are yet to find the "golden toilet," a friend of mine claims to have seen Machu Picchu while squatting in the grass next to the trail and says that the ancient city was framed by a rainbow! A once-in-a-lifetime experience...

Of all the characters in *Star Wars*, I think this loo looks most like an Ewok, or R2D2.

A Loo With a Cockatoo

View: unknown

In 2008, I was privileged to see a pair of green Indian ring-necked parakeets from the toilet window of a former Indian palace (p66). But not in my wildest dreams did I imagine that just a few months later I would be feasting my eyes on this astonishing scene.

Thanks to Australian-based animal trainer Trieste Visier for sending in this extraordinary image. I acknowledge that it's not technically a "loo with a view." But it is a loo with a budgie perched on top and that's good enough for me.

Trieste photographs budgerigars getting up to everyday antics, e.g. skateboarding, playing tennis and playing the guitar.

The budgie is clearly well trained and is doing a tremendous job of appearing constipated – an affliction said to be shared by Martin Luther, the father of the sixteenth-century Protestant Reformation. In 2004, archaeologists in Germany discovered his loo, where he reputedly spent many hours in quiet contemplation.

It was a toilet that helped change the world. Somehow, I think this one might change the world too.

Trieste's budgies can be seen at www.skateboardingbudgies.blogspot.com.

A View That Needs a Loo

Summit of Mount Fuji, Honshū, Japan

View: NOT from a toilet – "Fuji-San" casts its imperious shadow out west over Japan

FUJISAN-CHO POST OFFICE

Having climbed through the night to make it in time for sunrise, the summit of Mount Fuji was filled with glorious surprises – vending machines selling hot and cold drinks, a noodle restaurant, even a post office.

After enjoying a hot coffee from a can, purchased from a machine at nearly 4,000 meters (13,123 feet), and visiting the loo which I had traveled thousands of kilometers to see, I decided to walk round the crater rim before starting my descent. It takes about an hour and is a moment of calm in an otherwise grueling, albeit extraordinary, experience.

About halfway round, on the west side, the most excited man I have ever seen called me over and beckoned me up a ladder to a small viewing platform. PHEN-OM-EN-AL!

An awe-inspiring view, but where's the toilet to see it from?!
Can't believe that was the first thing that crossed my mind.

It's included to illustrate the highs and lows of hunting for loo-views.

(See p4 for more on the summit toilet.)

Chrysler Building [STATUS "MYTHICAL"]

Manhattan Island, New York City, New York, United States

View: 360-degree panoramas from golden toilet?

On a trip to New York City, I happened upon an urban legend. At the very top of the Chrysler Building and accessible only by a series of ladders (some even say it's inside the spire), supposedly sits a toilet! The story goes that the famous industrialist Walter P. Chrysler wanted the highest room in his building – once the tallest in the world – to be a toilet. Perhaps so he could sit and look out at the world he had conquered.

Following a chance meeting at a wedding, the plot thickened. Although most of the Chrysler Building is closed to the public, incredibly, someone knew someone who had seen this mythical latrine. They report that not only does it exist, but it also has 360-degree views of New York and is made of solid gold!

Part of me doesn't even want to know. What if it isn't true? However, if these incredible reports are confirmed, this would surely be the ultimate loo with a view. My search would be over and I could rest easy.

What a place it would be to end a journey.

Acknowledgments

I would like to thank everyone who has helped to make this book possible. Alone, my search would surely have been futile.

For their support and patience: my family; Hattie Wood; Anna and Matt Cardy; Joe Burns; Claudia Shaffer; Libby Mourant and Jon Hawkins.

Thanks to everyone who has contacted me with loo leads and photos.

To the team at Virgin Books, especially Ed Faulkner and Davina Russell.

To those who have shared their loo-view experiences with me, especially Irene Cahill and Ken Levan.

To English Heritage at Dover Castle; the legendary Wayan; the Copeland Bird Observatory; One Tree Island Research Station; TESFA; the Department of Conservation, New Zealand and the US National Park Service. To Howard Smith; Miyuki Kogi; Tom Henson; Kimberly Deni; Brendan Maguire; Brian McKeon; Chiaki Yamauchi; Isabel Ollivier; John Cantwell; Mike Fletcher; the Samli Family; Lesley Bellus; and many more.

But most of all, thanks to the loos – I couldn't have done it without you guys...

In no particular order, special thanks to: Anna, Matt and Ollie Cardy; Gabrielle Carter; Melanie Erlam; Jon Hawkins; Samuel Kashima; Mum and Dad, Sarah and Paul Barclay (Dad, you've been incredible, thanks from 'Lucas Old Boy'); Sourav Basu; Tom Henson; the owners of Cock View Manor; David Briese; Rhiannon May Jones; anyone involved in Outhouse Racing and whoever thought it up; Sophia Brown and Toby Clarke; The Tresco Estate; Alice Barclay; Ashanti Lodge Cape Town; budgies in general; The Landmark Trust; Grace Bastidas; Jacob Jones; Sarah and Matt Law; Lindsey Kucharski; the team at frost-sucks.org; Old Mondoro Bush Camp; Max, George and Bella; Tim Court; Wolwedans Lodge, Namibia; Airship Ventures; James Spackman; Lizzi Carter; The Renaissance Hotel, Pittsburgh; and many more...

I'd love to hear about any inspiring loo finds: loos@looswithviews.com

Photo Credits

Pages

2–3, 5 © Valerie McDougall; 6–11, 14–15, 20–21, 26–27, 30–33, 42–45, 54–55, 64–67, 72–73, 78–79, 87, 94–97, 108–109, 114–117, 140, 166, 168–169, 171 © Luke Barclay; 12–13 © Bryan Long; 16 © Arman Rin, Jr; 17 © David Gómez-Rosado and Lorena Fernández-Fernández, 2006; 18 © John Taggart; 19 © Cedric Babled; 22, 23, 76, 77 © Chris Belsten; 24 © Wendy Cue; 25 © Anna Maria S. Jorgensen; 28–29 © Nathan Thadani; 34 © Josh & Amber Johnson; 35 © Jocelyn King; 36, 37, 62, 63, 106, 124–125 © Anna Cardy; 38–39 © Neville McKee; 40–41 © Jennifer Reiffel; 46–47 © Hannah Woodthorpe; 48–49 © Maxime Renaudin; 50–51, 112–113 © Chris R Stokes; 52–53 © Adam Russell; 56–57 © Larry Mah; 58–59 © Kim Ollivier; 60–61 © Pat Baumann; 68–69, 86, 158–159 © David Briese; 70–71© Andrew Wooster; 74–75 © Emerald Huang; 80 © Susan Grant; 81 © Mark Chapman; 88–89 © Ryan Wong; 90 © Caroline Culbert, courtesy of Wilderness Safaris; 91 © Dana Allen, courtesy of Wilderness Safaris; 92–93, 156–157 © Diana and Bart-Willem van Leeuwen; 98–99© Sourav Basu; 100–101, 164–165 © Rhiannon May Jones*; 102–103 © Airship Ventures, Inc.; 104–105 © Samantha Cope; 107 © Robin Oakley; 110–111 © Jindrich Capek; 118–119 © Peter Brookes; 120–121 © Carol Hill; 122–123, 149 © David Hanmer; 126–127 © Burt Rosen; 128–129 © Andy Cunningham; 130–131 © Grace Bastidas; 133 © Jennifer Swayne; 84 © Maurizio Pichierri; 85 © Tracey Garrett; 134–135 © Sarah Law; 136–137 © Jane Thatcher; 138–139 © Richard Bottle; 141 © Henry Readhead; 143 © Sam Barclay; 144–145 © Jacob Jones; 146–147, 162–163 © Gabrielle Carter; 150–151 © David McLerran; 152–153 © Lana De Villiers; 154–155 © Terry Langhorn; 161 © Roger and Rosemary Tranter; 167 © Trieste Visier

* rhiannonmayphotography.co.uk

The Loo List